The Pathway to Positive Influence

Discover a New Way to Help Guide Those You Care About Most

Other books by David A. Esposito:

LOOKING BACK—What I Learned When I Left a Great Company
Lessons in Leadership to Help Senior Executives Win the War for Top Talent

Once a Week—52 small steps on a year-long journey to reach your full potential.

The Principles of Our World children's book series

All books are available on Amazon.com

Please visit www.harvesttimepartners.com for a current listing of books and resources.

The Pathway to Positive Influence

*Discover a New Way to Help
Guide Those You Care About Most*

David A. Esposito

Copyright © 2019
David Anthony Esposito
All rights reserved.

Independently published through Kindle Direct Publishing, an Amazon Company.
www.kdp.amazon.com

This book or any portion thereof may not be reproduced or used in any manner whatsoever without the express written permission of the author (David Anthony Esposito) except for the use of brief quotations in a book review.

For additional information and permissions, please contact:
Harvest Time Partners, Inc.
Attention: David Anthony Esposito
Email: david@harvesttimepartners.com

Harvest Time Partners, Inc.
ISBN-13: 978-0-578-45194-7
ISBN-10: 0-578-45194-8

DEDICATION

This book is dedicated to my mom, Mabel Leslie (Ballentyne) Esposito. She modeled the Pathway to Positive Influence her entire life…and continues to do so. Her positive influence has impacted countless numbers of people over the years. Thank you, Mom, for setting a wonderful example to follow.

CONTENTS

Acknowledgments ix

Introduction 1

Before We Begin: Intent 5

Step One: Open a door to THEIR STORY 13
- Listen
- Empathize

Step Two: Establish a genuine CONNECTION 25
- Share Experiences
- Share Learnings

Step Three: Discover new ways to SACRIFICE 39
- Serve
- Give
- Grace

Moving Forward 57
- Now, It's Your Turn
- A Worthy Message to Deliver
- Resources to Help

ACKNOWLEDGMENTS

I want to thank my wife Tracy and our four children, Stephanie, Samantha, David, and Jonathan. You have demonstrated some incredible patience as I have tried my hand at influence in a number of unproductive ways over the years. Your very loving and firm direct feedback has helped develop this Pathway to Positive Influence. ☺

I also want to thank Michael Piperno. Your ongoing support with my writing continues to give me the encouragement to take my turn venturing into the unknown.

INTRODUCTION

We all play a role in influencing those around us.

Whether we believe it or deny it, the truth remains that we have an influence on others. Our influence may have a positive or negative impact, or it may be simply dismissed through apathy or pre-judgment by the receiver.

Even when we leave this life, our influence remains in the thoughts and memories of those who knew us. Our legacy is the eternal impact of our influence during this life.

This book is intended to help those who desire to have a more positive influence on those they care about most at home, work, and in the community.

In today's world, often it is the *Loud and Proud* who seem to garner the most attention and drive the most influence. We are taught at a young age to speak up and share our point of view, broadcast our skills and accomplishments, and make sure our presence is felt. As adults, we read books on how to effectively present ourselves, outline our rationale, and effectively debate points of view to try and influence others. These loud and proud techniques have expanded their dominance as society moves through a fundamental shift in routine communications now primarily delivered electronically via social media.

The loud and proud methodology could not be less effective when you are trying to have a lasting, positive impact on others. The Pathway to Positive Influence will shine a light on the most effective way to have a positive influence on those we care about most.

The steps along the pathway are simple, yet difficult to do in the real world.

Most of us have been conditioned to feel that the loud and proud methodology is the best way to influence others. We speak first and tell people about our accomplishments and how experienced we are in order to "sell" them on listening to our point of view and embracing our thinking.

The Pathway to Positive Influence outlines steps that go against the hard-wiring of our environment. It places an initial emphasis on opening a door to the story of those we care to influence. It starts with them, not with us.

THE PATHWAY TO POSITIVE INFLUENCE

The outcome of staying engaged on the Pathway to Positive Influence will be seen in the lives of those we influence who will do more than they would ever have been able to do on their own. We will enable those we care about most to raise their own standards and reach their full potential. The Pathway to Positive Influence provides the steps to inspire others to make "our world" better in the home, workplace, and community.

At the end of our journey, we will not be reviewing our accomplishments or submitting our financial results. We will be staring into the eyes of those we influenced most.

At the end of our journey, we will not be reviewing our accomplishments or submitting our financial results. We will be staring into the eyes of those we influenced most. It is my hope that this new pathway helps you have a more positive influence on those you care about most and when you reach the end of your journey, you will have countless people standing around to say how grateful they are for your positive influence on them.

I hope you enjoy learning about this new pathway.

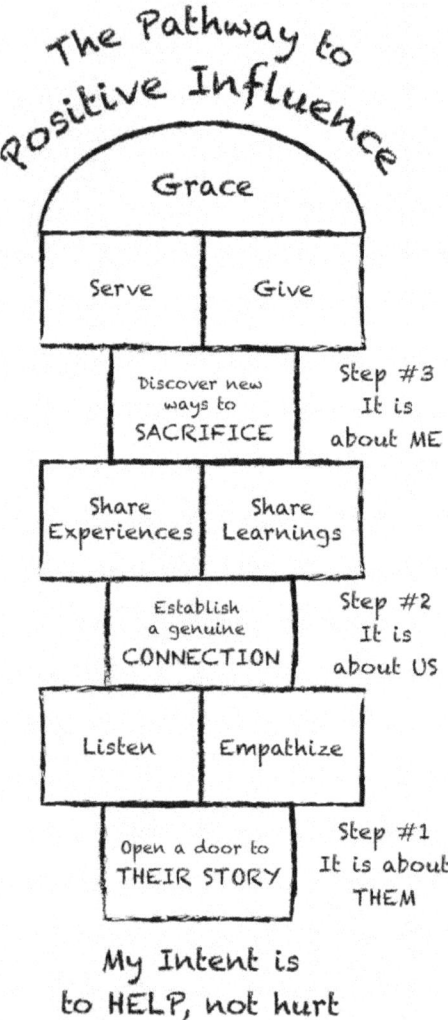

The Pathway to Positive Influence will be detailed in the subsequent chapters.

In addition, free copies of the pathway can be downloaded at harvesttimepartners.com

BEFORE WE BEGIN

Intent

Most of us will not be listed in the Hall of Fame of our chosen profession. Most of us will not be written about in the history books outlining the great innovators who changed the world. A few of us may be lucky enough to have our 15 minutes of fame.

However, we all cast some form of influence on those closest to us, those we care about most at home, at work, and in our community.

As we remain intentional and hopeful about reaching our full potential and having a positive impact on those around us, it is important that we learn and follow a well-established, principle-based Pathway to Positive Influence.

In our public world where the loud and proud get the most attention, this process may seem out of touch with the present reality. However, when we chronicle the archives of history in the home and in the public square, we will come to appreciate these steps as the most effective pathway to long-term, sustained positive influence on the lives of others, especially those we care about most.

Over the next sections of this book, we will journey together on a road less traveled in today's public forums and look closely at the most effective Pathway to Positive Influence.

The first step in any major effort to have influence is to examine our intent. When we look at the opportunity to have influence on others, what is our intent?

> Do we strive to influence others for our own personal gain, credit, or some hidden agenda? Is our desire to influence from a purely selfish motive?

> Or

> Do we strive to influence others based on a desire to help where we see a need? Do we want to help fill a gap in knowledge or skills created by youth, inexperience, or lack of awareness or resources? Do we simply care and want to help?

Examining our intent is the foundation for moving forward effectively on the Pathway to Positive Influence.

THE PATHWAY TO POSITIVE INFLUENCE

The pathway begins with a strong foundation where our intent is aligned with a desire to help, to serve, and to give to others. We have come to the humble realization that life is often difficult, and we all need some help along the way.

Those who desire to have a positive influence on others recognize that we all need some help along the way.

There are no "self-made" men and women. We don't live alone on an island. We have all received some help along the way. Whether it was encouragement at home, a positive role model on the field of play, advice from a friend or mentor, a stranger's kind offering, or a teacher from our past, we all have received some help. Those who desire to have a positive influence on others recognize that we all need some help along the way.

Our desire to have a positive influence on others begins with an intent to help and not to hurt.

One of the most consistent and critical situations for influence is as the role of parents and the desire to have a positive influence on our children. The methods of parental influence vary with age but suffice to say that most parental influence in early childhood is focused on setting the example through quiet modeling, showing and telling, and guiding with a loving hand as children gain some level of independence.

The role of parental influence begins to transition to more of a trusted guide and coach as adolescents and young adults begin to move into the uniqueness of their own creation. It is in those adolescent and young adult years that parents need to be especially self-aware of their intent and continue to remain focused on their intent to help, and not hurt.

In this most critical of life's roles, there are two common misguided intents that we all need to guard against.

If we are not careful, we as parents can frame our children as some sort of extension of our own personal scorecard or list of accomplishments.

Misguided Intent #1:

If we are not careful, we as parents can frame our children as some sort of extension of our own personal scorecard or list of accomplishments. We may succumb to our own insecurities and drive our children's accomplishment to compensate for our own shortcomings or to help boost our own self-image. The result is that our self-perceived intent to help our children is warped because we are just trying to have our kids accomplish more to support our own collection of trophies. When we do so, we harm our children's ability to fully embrace their own uniqueness and desire to be themselves. We should guide our children to become them, not us.

As parents, we need to closely guard against the temptation to push our adolescent and young adult children to accomplish our list of important things or become someone they are not in an attempt to fill gaps in our own insecurities. Those actions will most often drive a negative influence on our children and prevent them from reaching their own unique potential.

Misguided Intent #2:

For parents with more than one child, there is a strong tendency to over compensate for areas of common interest among our kids at the detriment of not fully embracing the unique abilities and desires of each child.

Quite often, if the first child develops into an athlete or musician, the other children follow suit. This can make logistics a lot easier for parents, but we all need to guard against "everyone enjoys the same things" mindset that may limit the creativity and uniqueness of all the children in the household.

Parents should remain attune to the tone and body language of children who may be screaming silently, "I am not like my sister or my brother!"

Many of these childhood pursuits are all well and good. It may be difficult to notice, but underneath a parent's self-perceived intent to help our children may be the parental desire for a smooth path of logistics, schedules, and financial considerations.

As we outline the steps along the Pathway to Positive Influence in the subsequent chapters, it is important to understand and appreciate a few key points:

(1) The desire to be a positive influence on those we care about most is a life-long pursuit. We can't expect to build a legacy of positive impact in one glorious interaction. We need to keep our eyes on the horizon guided by the true north of our intent to help, and simply keep moving forward.

(2) We can't expect a quick turn around and an open embrace to our new efforts to have a positive influence when we have a history of trying to cascade influence in a negative way. It will take time for those we care about most to not pre-judge our efforts to change our ways.

(3) Even though we are on a life-long journey to cast a positive influence, the process of moving through the steps of the Pathway to Positive Influence can occur in one interaction. When we have a genuine conversation with someone while sharing a meal or a long car ride, the pathway can guide us to a meaningful connection. We should be well equipped to travel the full pathway when the time and connection is available.

THE PATHWAY TO POSITIVE INFLUENCE

Continuing to examine our intent to ensure we are focused on helping those we care about most and minimizing the gravitational pull towards our own selfish motives is important as we begin to move down the Pathway to Positive Influence. We need to remain anchored on the foundation to help and not hurt.

STEP ONE

Open a door to THEIR STORY

"Be kind, for everyone you meet is fighting a hard battle." Plato (428–348 BC)

The first step along the Pathway to Positive Influence is to open a door to THEIR STORY.

Often in our world today, we are guided to be the first to talk, raise our voice, and quickly show others how smart we are, how accomplished we are, and how important a role we play in their lives.

The first, and most critical step, to have a lasting positive influence on others is to realize it is about them and NOT US. Our actions need to be focused on opening a door to their story. Everyone has a unique story to their lives. We should strive to understand it.

Understanding their story will help us determine how we can effectively help them. Again, our intent is to help, not hurt.

When we steamroll ourselves into others' lives, we close a door to learning about their uniqueness and fully understanding their struggles and victories, and their hopes and dreams. When we create an environment that closes a door vs. opens a door to their story, we limit our ability to have a positive influence.

In addition, it is important to remember that after we have the basics for survival, the greatest human need is to know that we matter to someone or some cause. When we create an environment that opens a door to their story, we demonstrate that they matter to us. We meet a clear and present emotional need in them by opening a door to THEIR STORY.

THE PATHWAY TO POSITIVE INFLUENCE

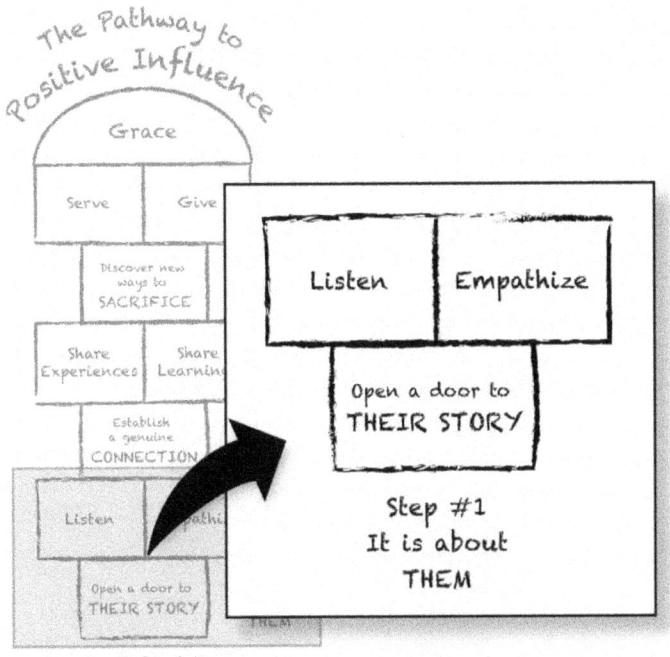

Listen

*"We have two ears and one tongue so that
we would listen more and talk less."*
Diogenes (412–323 BC)

One of the helpful ways to open a door to their story is to simply listen.

In a world that emphasizes talking over listening and often rewards the loudest person in the room, listening seems like an activity for the weak and feeble. Listening goes against the popular opinion that we need to be up front and on stage with our intelligence and experience in order to have influence. However, listening is the most thoughtful and effective means to begin to understand someone else.

The reality is much different than the popular public perception of influence. We need to initially focus on listening instead of talking to most effectively move forward in having a positive influence on others.

We send a huge billboard-sized message that says, "You are not that important to me" when we show up to listen and we are constantly "stepping out" of conversation with the casual glance at notifications on our phone.

Given the overwhelming emphasis in our world to talk rather than listen, below are some additional points to encourage all of us to be more effective at listening so we can open a door to their story:

(1) **No effective response needed.** Many of us hinder our ability to effectively listen because we have been conditioned that to have a positive impact on others, we need to know what to say and prepare an effective response while we are in conversation with them. It may sound counterintuitive, but we need to focus all of our energy on listening with the hope to understand instead of listening with a desire to respond with something "brilliant." If we don't initially focus on listening, our "brilliant" response will most often fall on deaf ears or be completely irrelevant to the situation.

(2) **Ask additional questions in follow-up.** Thoughtful questions followed by a learned discipline to be silent will help encourage others to keep sharing. Asking a follow-up question and simply shutting up can be difficult but allowing silence to hang after a question will open the door for others to fill the gap and continue to share. Even something as simple as, "Please tell me a little more about that experience" or "It seems like there is still something that is bothering you" or "Please share a little more to help me better understand what you are going through" can keep the discussion going in an effective direction.

(3) **Focus on him/her, not everything else in "my" world.** In today's massively distracted world, keeping smart phones, laptops, etc. out of sight will help send a message that the focus is on them and not anything else. We send a huge billboard-sized message that says, "You are not that important to me" when we show up to listen and we are constantly "stepping out" of conversation with the casual glance at notifications on our phone. Our ability to positively influence others will be severely limited when we allow simple distractions to creep into our attempt to listen.

(4) **We don't need to be brilliant to listen, we just need to care.** Listening, not talking, is the

most simple and powerful way to demonstrate to someone that they matter and to meet a human desire to be accepted for who we are today. Listening is the gateway to truth in a conversation and can encourage others, at least for a moment, to take their mask off and end the "costume party" we all typically live in.

As we continue to strive to open a door to someone's story, listening instead of talking will help keep the door open and keep us on the Pathway to Positive influence.

Some questions for deeper reflection:

When was the last time you simply spoke too much instead of listening and you could tell your actions closed a door to learn more about the other person?

When was the last time you let your mind wander when you were talking one on one with someone?

How do you feel when others glance down at their phone when they are talking to you?

What example around listening are you consistently setting when you sit one on one with someone?

THE PATHWAY TO POSITIVE INFLUENCE

Empathize

"One of the most beautiful qualities of true friendship is to understand and to be understood." Seneca (4 BC–65 AD)

Another helpful way to open a door to THEIR STORY is to empathize and try to walk in their shoes.

Empathy is about seeing experiences from the lens of others, understanding their perspective, and feeling what they feel.

None of us see the world as it is. We see the world from our own unique perspective. That is a critical element to improve our level of self-awareness and encourage us to work hard to understand others. We see the world as we are, not as it is.

If I were to ask you what the American flag means to

you, I would hear a multitude of responses. They would all be responses based on your lens of experience, not mine. Empathy helps me understand your response a little better.

If I were to ask you about the rising rates, across all age groups, of mental illness in our country, I would hear a multitude of responses and a different perspective from:

- Those who personally struggle with depression, anxiety, etc.

- Sons and daughters who had a parent struggle with mental health and perhaps covered it with alcohol or drugs.

- Parents who struggled to help a child walk through depression.

- Children who lost a parent to post-traumatic stress disorder (PTSD).

- Adult children caring for a parent with dementia or Alzheimer's.

- Those who have not been directly and personally impacted by mental illness.

Empathy helps me expand my ability to see what you see, understand you better, and feel what you feel.

THE PATHWAY TO POSITIVE INFLUENCE

Empathy is not a natural, easy skill for many of us. Most of us are hard-wired to be a bit selfish, focused on our own needs, and to view the world only from our perspective. We need to be intentional and disciplined to continue to grow our empathy towards others. Below are a few additional thoughts to encourage all of us to focus on empathy as an important component to opening a door others' stories:

(1) People desire to be understood in their own uniqueness. Empathy helps us avoid oversimplifying life and placing people in pre-judged buckets like "rich/poor," "smart/ignorant," "city-street smart/country hick," "self-made/silver spoon," etc.

(2) Instead of projecting our own story on others and making assumptions and interpretations about them, empathy helps us get into the heart and soul of those around us.

(3) Empathy is very difficult to achieve over a text message. It's most effectively embraced when we listen not just with our ears but focus our eyes, heart, and physical presence with another person.

As we continue to strive to open a door to someone's story, focusing on empathy instead of projecting our view on others and assuming everyone shares a similar reality, will help to keep the door open and keep us on the Pathway to Positive Influence.

Some questions for deeper reflection:

When was the last time you sat with someone and listened as they described a particular situation and you could genuinely feel what they were going through?

Can you remember the last time you wept openly with another person? What was the situation, and can you describe the depth of meaning you felt because of the experience?

What experiences in your past make it difficult for you to empathize with others?

STEP TWO

Establish a genuine CONNECTION

Our relationships give life purpose and direction.

The second step along the Pathway to Positive Influence is to establish a genuine CONNECTION.

Life is to be lived in relationship with others. Isolation gives rise to a host of physical and mental health problems. Whether we are an introvert or extrovert, we need to be in relationship with others to reach our full potential. As we move into the second step on the pathway and work to create a genuine connection, we realize that it is not about me or you, it is about US.

Once we open a door to THEIR STORY in the first step, we are now ready to discover some common experiences and share some learnings that will begin to create a willing heart that is receptive to influence. As we share these common experiences and learnings, we will begin to build trust, which is critical to sustain a genuine, healthy connection with others.

In our world there are some who will attempt to build relationships solely for personal gain. As we look to be a positive influence on those around us, we need to ensure our intent remains anchored on the foundation to help and work hard to avoid being overcome by some hidden selfish agenda.

Establishing a genuine connection is built on trust and a sincere desire for an authentic, shame-free, and judgment-free relationship.

THE PATHWAY TO POSITIVE INFLUENCE

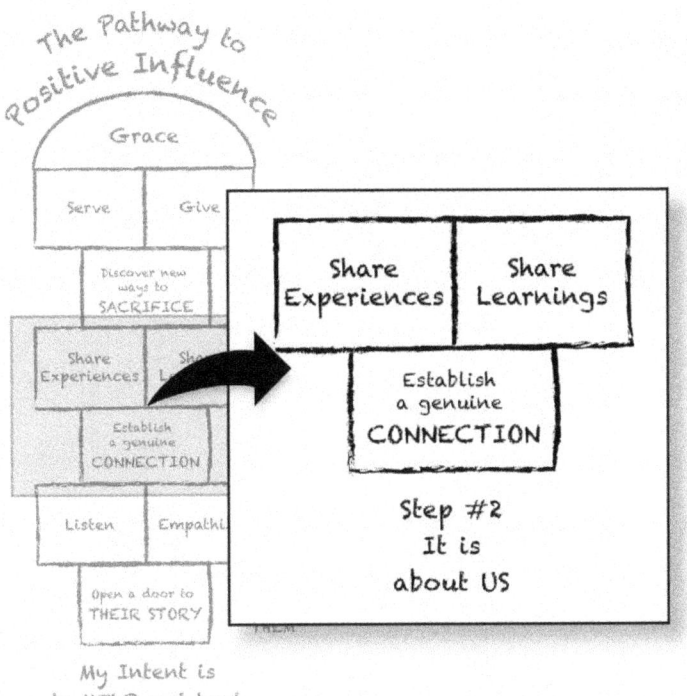

Share Experiences

"The journey of a thousand miles begins with one step." Lao Tzu (601–530 BC)

We all share some common experiences in our journey of life. As a result of these experiences, we often share similar emotions through the experience of failure and success, fear and worry during difficult times, and joy and peace during uplifting times. As we look to establish a genuine connection with others, sharing common experiences and the emotions surrounding those experiences can create the real connection we desire and the establishment of trust that supports our journey on the Pathway to Positive Influence.

There is often no greater connection that can be made with someone than sharing a common experience and the emotions that accompany it. Those who fear public speaking can readily connect to someone nervously getting ready to stand in front of a crowd. Those who may have had a most difficult journey through adolescence can readily connect with a teenager experiencing feelings of loneliness, isolation, and rejection. Those who have endured the pain and sadness of the breakup of a family are in a good position to relate to someone walking alone out of a broken relationship.

Discovering some common experiences and shared emotions is often helpful to build a connection to someone and create an open heart for influence. Those who have endured a specific experience are very often the most helpful to relate to the needs of those dealing with a similar experience.

Below are a few additional thoughts to encourage all of us to look for common experiences and the shared emotions around those experiences in order to establish a genuine connection that will enable an openness for positive influence:

(1) We have a tendency (especially men) to be hesitant about sharing emotions. As we look to establish a genuine connection, we need to be courageous and proactive in sharing some common emotions that many may be less willing to share like fear, sadness, and shame. As we set an example, we encourage others to come forward with some of these more difficult emotions. Many of us try to deal with

difficult emotions alone, which is consistently proven to be the least effective way to heal. When we share, we may help others come forward and address these underlying emotions in a healthier and more productive way.

(2) Many of us move further into isolation when we are in periods of suffering and hardship. We prefer to suffer alone for a variety of reasons. As we continue to demonstrate an openness to share a difficult experience and/or a current struggle, our example can help open the door for someone to ask for help in a genuine area of need and be receptive to the positive influence of others.

Most of us don't have much trouble sharing our uplifting experiences and successes. However, experience tells us that sharing successes does not routinely foster the genuine, authentic connection we are striving for in being a positive influence.

It is quite often the painful experiences and the difficult emotions that are most guarded in our relationships. However, when we share painful experiences and difficult emotions, experience tells us that we create the genuine connection that prepares the heart for influence. We should strive to be courageous and set the example of being open to share in the hope that those who are hurting in silence can now speak and receive help. In the process, we will establish a genuine connection along the Pathway to Positive Influence.

One additional point about close relationships and sharing experiences needs to be addressed. For close relationships that have become strained over the years, as is common in marriage or between grown children and their parents, sharing experiences and emotions can be most helpful in our attempts to heal. As we share thoughts on the experiences that most likely caused the strain in the relationship, it is not productive to simply label the other person by saying things like:

"You did this because you are a selfish jerk."

"You are the most stubborn person."

"You still act like a spoiled brat."

"You have no clue how rude you are to me."

"Given all I have done for you, you are still just ungrateful and lazy."

A much more productive way to describe the experiences would be to simply describe how they made us feel. For example:

"When you do things like _____, it makes me feel unloved."

"When you consistently act this way, it makes me feel worthless and I can't do anything right."

"When you talk over me, it makes me feel like I am a child again and my big sister is dominating the discussion."

"When you say _____, it makes me feel like you don't even realize how tough things are for me right now."

"I lose hope for our relationship when you continue to _____."

When we describe how these experiences make us feel, it has been proven to help open a door to a more productive discussion as opposed to the same things over and over again before we just quit trying. What do we have to lose to try something different?

As we look to create a heart for influence and improve a troubled close relationship, we will most likely need to try something different.

Some questions for deeper reflection:

When was the last time you shared a difficult experience and painful emotions with someone? What was the situation and what was the result of sharing?

Can you remember a time when someone close to you shared a painful experience? How did the sharing come about and what happened as a result?

What holds you back from sharing some difficult experiences with those you care about most? What would it take for you to be more open to share?

THE PATHWAY TO POSITIVE INFLUENCE

Share Learnings

"Experience is the teacher of all things."
Julius Caesar (100–44 BC)

How we use our experiences will determine our future potential. If we use our experiences to learn and grow, we will reach our highest potential. If we use our experiences to remind us of our shortcomings or wallow in our mistakes, we will limit our effectiveness and our impact on those around us.

Another important element to further establish a genuine connection along the Pathway to Positive Influence is to share learnings from our common experiences.

Wisdom comes with time, experience, and, most importantly, through intentional reflection to discover some learnings from our life's journey. Imparting wisdom based on learnings across some of our common life experiences is at the heart of positive influence.

The passing on of wisdom from generation to generation (wise old folks to the young and naïve) and from the learned journeyman to those who do not currently possess the mental or emotional capacity to learn and grow ("This is just the way I am," "You can't teach an old dog new tricks," "This is the way I was raised") is where the Pathway to Positive Influence has its greatest opportunity to impact the lives of others.

Effectively sharing learnings (imparting wisdom) is a two-way street. There needs to be a willing teacher and a willing student. As we have established an open door and a genuine connection, we are now best positioned to share learnings and have a positive influence in our day-to-day relationships.

The principle of humility is an effective guardrail as we begin to effectively share learnings from our experience. No one responds well to an arrogant windbag. Learnings gained through the crucible of experience are most effectively shared and received by adhering to the principle of humility.

Below are a few additional ideas around sharing learnings in order to move forward along the Pathway to Positive Influence:

(1) **Growth vs. Limitations:** There is a clear

difference among people in the area of learning from experience. Some of us view past experiences as opportunities to learn and grow while others use past experiences to reinforce some perceived limitation and shortcoming. The truth is that we reach our full potential when we view past experiences as opportunities to learn and grow. It may take some time for someone to acknowledge and accept that truth. Be understanding.

(2) **Seeds of Wisdom:** Learnings are best shared and received over time in bite-sized chunks as opposed to a massive flood all at once. The Pathway to Positive Influence is a long journey with no shortcuts or an EZ-Pass to accelerate the process. Accept the reality that planting seeds and adhering to the truth contained in the law of the harvest—it takes time, intention, effort, and faith to reap an abundant harvest, or in this case, a legacy of positive influence on those we care about most. Be patient.

(3) **Remember the Past:** As we share learnings in the hope to inspire others, we should take time to consistently reinforce their prior experiences of overcoming, persevering, and moments of joy. Helping others remember these uplifting experiences can be an encouragement to open their heart and enable additional learning and growth. Be reflective.

When we thoughtfully and humbly share learnings from some common experiences, we begin to create the environment where shared learnings can bring about positive behavior change and help others to reach their full potential.

Some questions for deeper reflection:

Describe a time when you received some wisdom from an older person. What was the wisdom they shared?

When was the last time you gained some genuine insight from an experience and tried to share it with those you care about most? What happened and what was the result?

How do you view prior difficult experiences…as opportunities to grow or a reinforcement of your shortcomings? Why do you hold to that point of view?

STEP THREE

Discover new ways to SACRIFICE

"There is no greater love than to lay down one's life for one's friends." (John 15:13-15)

To lay down our life on the altar of sacrifice is the greatest of all actions to drive a positive influence on others and to ensure a legacy we desire. As we sacrifice our self-interests and egos, overcome our insecurities and hesitations, and begin to focus our efforts on others, we create the habits necessary to remain steadfast on the Pathway to Positive Influence.

During the first step along the pathway, we opened a door to THEIR STORY. It was about THEM, not us. The second step along the Pathway to Positive Influence enabled an open discussion around sharing experiences and the learnings from those experiences. Through sharing, we established a genuine CONNECTION. It was not about you or me, it was about US.

As we move to the third step in the pathway, we now know a great deal about those we care about most. We have listened and become empathetic to their story, not totally consumed with ours. We have built trust as we have established a genuine, authentic connection to each other and opened our hearts for influence as we began to share some wisdom gained from experience.

Step three on the Pathway to Positive Influence is about ME and the sacrifices I will make to help you based on all that I have discovered during our relationship together. I now know your story and where I can help. The time is now for me to act, to sacrifice and be consistent with my intent to help and not to hurt.

As we sacrifice our time, talent, and energy in support of those we care about most, we continually strengthen the bond of relationships that are vital to a healthy, fulfilling life.

There are three, proven areas of sacrifice that can help create the momentum for ongoing positive influence. The three areas for sacrifice are: Serve, Give, and Grace. When our sacrifice is anchored on these three actions, we create the continuous positive influence on those we care about most that will produce the legacy we hope to build.

THE PATHWAY TO POSITIVE INFLUENCE

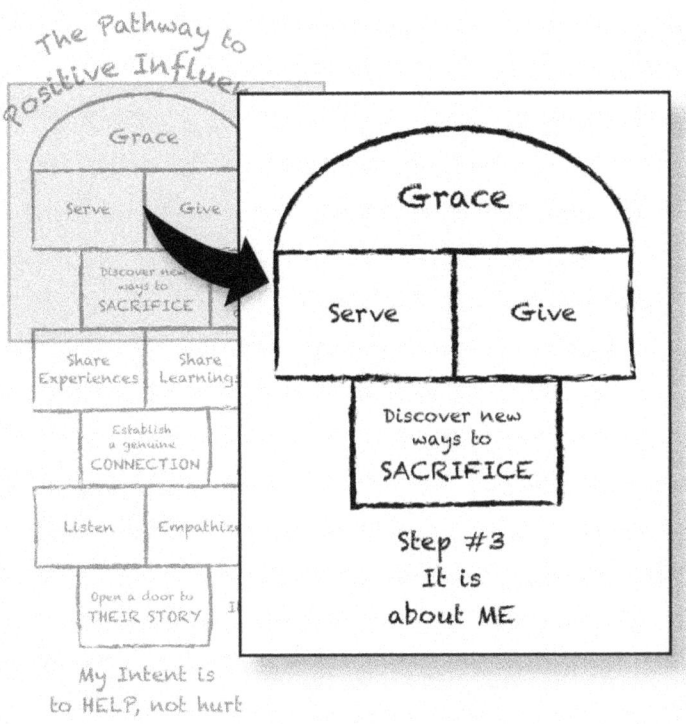

Serve

"The best way to find yourself is to lose yourself in the service of others." Mahatma Gandhi (1869–1948)

When we consistently act in the service of others and a cause greater than ourselves, we set an encouraging example for others to follow. The quiet servant, far from the headlines, focused on consistently moving the cause forward through the dark uncertain valleys, will more times than not cast a positive influence on those around them.

All of those with incredible intelligence, those with a loud voice, and those well-polished speakers eventually lose their luster through time and distance, but those who remain steadfast to serve others leave a legacy of positive impact that we would all cherish.

Our ability to have a positive influence throughout life's ups and downs can be most assured when we focus our efforts on serving others, especially those closest to us in our home.

It is important that we come to terms with the practical reality that close relationships are not easy. Life is complicated and often messy. Our ability to have a positive influence throughout life's ups and downs can be most assured when we focus our efforts on serving others, especially those closest to us in our home.

Below are a few points to help encourage all of us as we look to serve those we care about most.

(1) Life is hard and we could all use some help (help in tough times, and also help to push us to reach our full potential). By serving others we can be best positioned to help those in need who often may be hesitant to admit and accept some assistance.

(2) We typically serve in areas of our strengths. As we learn more about the needs of others, we may be called to serve in an area of need that is not our strength and may be difficult. Regardless, we should act in a manner that resonates with those we care about most, even if it is not our strength or "favorite" thing to do. Serving

those we care about most should be guided by the question "What needs to be done?" instead of "What do I like to do?"

(3) Serving others is what brings purpose, meaning, and lasting joy to our lives. When we simply focus on a search for our own happiness, we end up on an endless, insatiable quest. In our effort to serve others, we will find the lasting peace that can carry us through the moments of happiness and sorrow that accompany the normal cycles of life.

All of us, at certain points in our attempt to serve others for the long haul, will feel underappreciated for our efforts. Whether it is an ungrateful family member, an insensitive spouse, an adolescent going through that "know it all" phase, or a constantly complaining coworker, we all will go through times of serving where we just feel underappreciated and wonder if it is worth it.

In most cases, especially in the home, the tide does eventually turn. The insensitive spouse or the "know it all" adolescent eventually has that "light bulb" moment when they realize the quiet service that has been delivered faithfully over the years. However, if they do not, it is important that we do not lose our drive to deliver on our commitments and sacrifice to meet their needs. Continuing to move forward in quiet service is simply the right thing to do and sets a strong example for others to follow.

Some questions for deeper reflection:

Describe an example of someone you know who models the way for serving others? What do you find inspiring about their example?

When have you felt totally spent on serving others and seemed to have nothing remaining to carry on? What have you learned from that experience?

When was the last time you thanked someone for going out of their way to serve you?

Give

"For it is in giving that we receive." Francis of Assisi (1181–1226)

There is truth to the age-old adage that it is better to give than receive.

As we give in a meaningful way to others, we create the environment for a lasting positive influence.

Similar to serving, when we attempt to give to others, we have a strong tendency to give in areas that are meaningful to us but may not be as meaningful to the recipient. For example, some of us are overjoyed with the gift of encouragement because we need a little cheering on to keep moving forward with our life. Others may be grateful for the unexpected and thoughtful gift of a nice card or terrific meal. While still others are emotionally filled with just some quality time with those we care about most.

Our challenge is to discover and then deliver on that most meaningful area to give to those we care about most. Continually giving in an area that is desired by us, but not by someone else, will many times go unnoticed and underappreciated. In relationships that have become strained, the very act of giving in an area that is not meaningful and relevant to the recipient, can often make the situation worse. As we move through the initial steps on the pathway, we should gain a good sense as to the unique ways that someone would welcome our efforts to give.

We need to remain observant and intentional about uncovering the needs of others. As we all journey through different phases of life, our needs will change, and we need to continue to be open to give in various ways to meet the evolving needs of those we care about most. The idea of giving is not to create dependency but to demonstrate a willingness to sacrifice to give and support the needs of others. The act of giving will help to build a lasting legacy of positive impact on others.

Quite often as children grow and develop into adults, parents may lack the skills and experience to specifically coach and guide in some experiences in life that new generations encounter. One of the most underrated elements of giving is to simply offer a word of encouragement. When in doubt, encouragement can consistently fill a gap in all other areas of giving. Life is often difficult and most of us need a little encouragement along the way. It can provide several benefits:

(1) Encouragement reminds us that someone is interested in us and our present situation.

(2) Encouragement demonstrates that someone believes in our potential. In a world with a natural bent toward the negative, encouragement helps all of us refocus on a positive point of view, which consistently proves to be the differentiator between people achieving goals and those who fall short.

(3) Encouragement reminds us that we should have high expectations. Many times, we can let self-doubt and fear steal our potential to do great things. Encouragement helps us fix our eyes on the unlimited potential we have to make a difference in this world.

As we look to give more than receive in the relationships with those we care about most, we continue to cascade a positive influence on others.

Some questions for deeper reflection:

When was the last time you were the recipient of someone's generosity? What was it that you received and how did it make you feel?

What are some of the different ways of giving that are meaningful to those closest to you? How similar or different are they from the ways you like to give?

When was the last time you could tell that your way of giving to someone was not having the desired impact on them? How did you feel and what did you do about it?

Grace

"No one is useless in this world who lightens the burdens of another." Charles Dickens (1812–1870)

There is a reason that grace is on the top of the Pathway to Positive Influence.

With grace, we give people a second chance.

Grace is the most meaningful day-to-day sacrifice as we look to build lasting relationships with those we care about most. Grace, in essence, is providing redemption to someone even when all indications are that they don't deserve it. With an act of grace, we return favor to someone who in the practical view of the world, does not deserve it. With grace, we give people a second chance.

We see this second chance being played out many times in public although very few times is it called out specifically as a defining way to live in relationship with others. Here are just a few examples to bring meaning to the importance of grace and its lasting impact on building healthy relationships:

(1) After serving 27 difficult years in prison, Nelson Mandela emphasized reconciliation as an important component of his platform as the newly elected president of South Africa. He was accompanied by many of his former prison guards at his inauguration as an example of reconciliation. He knew if he held on to bitterness for the acts that they committed on him, he would not be totally free.

(2) Pope John Paul II was shot and wounded in an attempted assassination in May of 1981. The Pope later forgave his assassin and the Pope's request to pardon him was granted by the president of Italy. The Pope was a model of grace in an extreme situation.

(3) Numerous movie stars, rock stars, and athletes who humbly acknowledge mistakes and ask the public for forgiveness are consistently afforded grace and a second chance.

THE PATHWAY TO POSITIVE INFLUENCE

For those closest to us, grace means we simply don't quit on them.

Our culture is built on the desire to give people a second chance. We all know we can occasionally stumble. For those closest to us, grace means we simply don't quit on them. This commitment to not quit on someone builds the habits for positive influence over time.

If we have lived more than few days in relationship with others, we probably have seen our fair share of mistakes. Some mistakes were done to us and some mistakes we did to others. We all wish close relationships were easy, but the truth is, they are not.

Mistakes in relationships are sometimes lighthearted, but they can bring about a great deal of pain. As with most things in life, we have a few choices about how to respond to mistakes. How we choose our response when others make mistakes can help or hurt our efforts to have a positive influence on those we care about most.

For most of us, we have learned that remaining bitter and angry for a long period of time after mistakes does not particularly help the situation. Bitterness has been proven to result in greater pain and problems for all involved. In addition, the one who holds onto bitterness usually suffers the most compared to the one who first stumbled and fell short.

When we sacrifice our human, practical desire to punish the mistakes of others and instead redeem them with the power of grace, we deliver on the most effective way to rise above and many times, permanently solidify a positive influence on those we care about most. We rebuild a sense of belonging and acceptance when we demonstrate grace through communicating redemption towards an individual who made a mistake.

The act of "clearing" one's debt or "saving" someone from the continual pain and isolation of a poor choice and communicating our willingness to trust again is probably the greatest sacrificial challenge we will face in terms of building strong and healthy relationships after a mistake.

Providing redemption from past mistakes, as opposed to remaining bitter, has been shown time and again to build a strong sense of belonging and connection to those closest to us and cascade a most positive influence on others.

Some questions for deeper reflection:

Describe a time when someone close to you demonstrated grace after a mistake? How did it make you feel?

In what way are you still holding on to some bitterness or anger to someone who treated you poorly or made a mistake that impacted you in a negative way?

THE PATHWAY TO POSITIVE INFLUENCE

What is holding you back from demonstrating grace to someone who has hurt you…especially someone close to you?

MOVING FORWARD

Now, It's Your Turn

In a very predictable and traditional fashion, at the conclusion of every personal development book, presentation, video seminar, or pump-up speech, there comes a call to action, and we must decide what we are going to do next.

Well, now it is your turn to decide.

Most of us have observed the traditional form of influence in our society. Get a big megaphone and tell a great story about our background and experience in a manner that will motivate people to make a difference in their lives and the lives of others. This more traditional form of influence often has a positive impact in the short term. People either get emotionally engaged and motivated to change or they get turned off quickly because of some pre-judgement and perhaps jaded view of the world. However, even when the loud and proud method is successful in driving change, the impact has been proven to be short lived.

The Pathway to Positive Influence is a different approach and puts the other person at the center of the story, not us. The mindset shift is significant compared to examples we see all around us. The priority is on the other person and getting to know their story first, not tell them ours. We show interest in them first. As President Theodore Roosevelt Jr. famously said, "People don't care how much you know until they know how much you care."

If we look back over our lives, the examples of people who have a sustained positive influence on us are the ones who first cared about us.

As stated earlier in the book, the outcome of staying engaged on the Pathway to Positive Influence will be seen in the lives of those we influence who will do more than they would ever have been able to do on their own. We will enable those we care about most to raise their own standards and reach their full potential. The Pathway to Positive Influence provides the steps to inspire others to make "our world" better in the home, workplace, and community.

Now, it is your turn to use the pathway to guide those you care about most.

THE PATHWAY TO POSITIVE INFLUENCE

We have all made mistakes when trying to guide those we care about most.

One last point needs to be made as you determine your next step. We have all made mistakes when trying to guide those we care about most. Most of us have tried to steamroll our point of view either by brute force example over the years, continuing to say the same things over and over again (repetition builds retention, right?), or consistently failing to listen while we just kept talking. Please do not let the mistakes of the past and the damage they may have caused prevent you from climbing back into the ring to try and have a positive influence on those you care about most. By adhering to the pathway outlined in the book, you can have a measurable positive impact on their lives, and they need it now more than ever. Just start fresh by shutting up and listening and it will lead to a better place.

A Worthy Message to Deliver

We have all been around a few people in this world who have had a positive influence on us. Whether it was a family member, friend, teacher, coach, co-worker, or boss. Those people deserve to hear about the positive influence they had in our lives…and please allow me to be blunt, they need to hear from you before their funeral. Don't wait to just give a wonderful eulogy about their impact on you. Tell them before it is too late.

By delivering this worthy message to those who had a positive influence on us, we accomplish a few important things:

(1) Our message will be an encouraging voice of support to them as they, like all of us at some point, yearn to know if we matter to those we care about most. Our message to them will meet this most important human need to know

they did matter to others in this life.

(2) Our message will build momentum around having a positive influence on others in this world. They will receive this message warmly and will be energized to continue their positive influence on others. We also will be motivated to follow their example and work to have a positive influence on others just the way they were a help to us.

(3) Our message has the potential to re-open a door to a relationship that may have become cold over the years. Especially in the home, where family conflict is the most heartbreaking of all of life's struggles, just providing a message that someone had a positive influence on us may help to create a soft opening to what has become a troubled relationship.

(4) Our message will re-ignite the spark in the eyes of old folks. In the typical cycle of life, older parents begin to see themselves as a bit distant from the day-to-day, busy lives of their children and grandchildren. Delivering this message of positive influence to older family members can be an encouragement to re-ignite purpose and meaning in their life at a time when they don't always see themselves as contributing in a meaningful way anymore. It has been proven time and again that living a life of meaning and purpose, even in very old age,

plays a huge role in preventing disease, strengthening mental health, and is effective in minimizing the effects of conditions like Alzheimer's and dementia. When we have purpose and meaning, we choose to keep learning, growing, and living.

Our message is worthy to deliver and will build hope for the future.

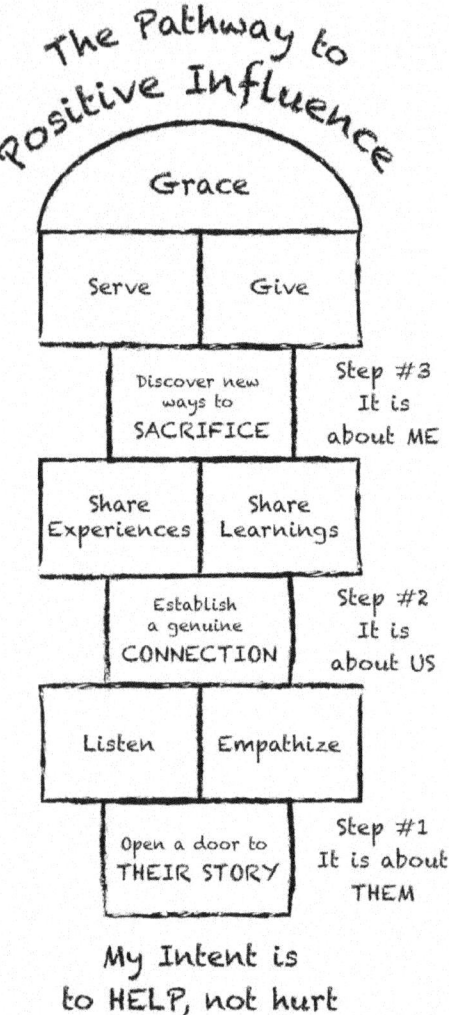

Free copies of the Pathway to Positive Influence can be downloaded at www.harvesttimepartners.com

Resources to Help

Let's face it, relationships are not easy. Especially the relationships we care about most at home, work, and in our community.

I wrote this book with the intent to help you have a positive influence on those you care about most to help them reach their full potential. I hope you found some relevant and insightful information to help you in your journey.

Please visit our website at harvesttimepartners.com as we have some additional resources to help.

Also, please feel free to contact me anytime. I would welcome the chance to connect and get to know each other better.

Mobile phone: 269-370-9275

Email: david@harvesttimepartners.com

I wish you all the best in reaching your full potential and having a positive influence on those you care about most.

David Esposito

ADDITIONAL RESOURCES FROM HARVEST TIME PARTNERS

Reality: We all struggle to have difficult conversations around the important things in life with those we care about most.

Face to Face

A unique set of resources to support families, educators, and counselors in opening a door to more effective communication about real-world, difficult issues and encouraging face-to-face discussion to improve decision-making and relationships. Available for various ages.

DAVID A. ESPOSITO

Abundant Harvest for Kids and Abundant Harvest for Teens & Adults

A patented, award-winning board game to support effective communication, reinforce principle-based decision making, and the Law of the Harvest. Simply, you reap what you sow.

THE PATHWAY TO POSITIVE INFLUENCE

The Principles of Our World Children's Book Series

It is never too early in the development of a child to start talking about the importance of principles like compassion, honesty, courage, and teamwork. *The Principles of Our World* books provide parents and teachers with the opportunity to teach children how **The Principles** can help them in a variety of situations they will experience in life.

For more information and to order these resources, go to www.harvesttimepartners.com

ABOUT THE AUTHOR

David is a combat veteran, business executive, husband, father, and creator of character-building resources that help individuals and families reach their full potential in an uncertain world.

After launching his business career as a sales representative, David quickly rose through the ranks of corporate America, advancing to the position of president and chief executive officer of several innovative healthcare companies that have made significant contributions in areas such as the early detection of cancer and allergic disease. David continues to be active in the healthcare marketplace as a strategic advisor to leadership teams building companies to lead the next wave of innovation in healthcare.

David's character and leadership skills were cultivated at West Point and through leadership assignments in the US Army Infantry. As a young infantry officer, David led a rifle platoon of 38 men with the 101st Airborne Division through several combat operations in the Gulf War. He was recognized with a Bronze Star for combat operations in February 1991.

David develops programs and resources designed to strengthen the character of individuals and build and sustain healthy relationships. This includes Character Creates Opportunity®, an initiative that was specifically designed to improve the character development of children, adolescents, and adults. David's patented, award-winning conversation game, Abundant Harvest®, is played by families, schools, counseling programs, and faith-based organizations worldwide as it opens a door to more productive dialogue and encourages decision making based on principles such as honesty, loyalty, and commitment. Reinforcing the Law of the Harvest, the game's primary lesson is the age-old adage that you will always reap what you sow. David also have created a conversation card game called Face to Face® that helps to foster effective conversations on real-world issues and to develop the critical life skill of face-to-face communication in a world that is rapidly changing how people connect.

David holds an MBA from Syracuse University and a bachelor's degree in civil engineering from West Point. He has appeared on CBS, NPR, and PBS and has been featured by many other news outlets.

THE PATHWAY TO POSITIVE INFLUENCE

David is available to provide support to business leaders, individuals, and organizations on a variety of topics, encompassing personal and executive development, leadership training, and building a strong marriage and family.

For more information on David and Harvest Time Partners, Inc., please visit harvesttimepartners.com

www.ingramcontent.com/pod-product-compliance
Lightning Source LLC
Chambersburg PA
CBHW020950090426
42736CB00010B/1350